Including Children with DCD/Dyspraxia in the Foundation Stage

Written by
Sharon Drew

Illustrated by
Martha Hardy

Including Children with Autistic Spectrum Disorders

ISBN 1 9050 1945 9

©Featherstone Education Ltd, 2005
Text © Sharon Drew 2005
Featherstone Education Ltd.
Illustrations © Martha Hardy 2005

First published in the UK, December 2005

Published in the United Kingdom by
Featherstone Education Ltd.
44 - 46 High Street
Husbands Bosworth
Leicestershire
LE17 6LP

Featherstone
Education

Contents

Including children with Developmental Co-ordination Disorder (DCD)/Dyspraxia in the Foundation Stage

The Foundation Stage is a time when children develop their knowledge and understanding of the world by exploring their environment through movement and developing independence skills. They now want to play with other children and make friends.

During this time they learn to:

- control their body as it moves - gauging pressure strength and speed;
- co-ordinate their bodies;
- understand the language of following instructions;
- plan their learning and organise themselves in their environment;
- develop adequate timing and rhythm in their movements to aid sequencing and repetition;
- be still;
- be aware of their environment and others.

This book:

This book considers children with Developmental Co-ordination Disorders (DCD)/Dyspraxia and how this condition can affect a child's ability to master and enjoy movement for play and learning.

The book offers some ABCs of DCD:

Advice
Background information
Current views
Developmental approach
Educational value
Fun activities
Good practice

Who is this book for?

The book is for anyone involved in the day to day care of young children. It will be of particular interest to early years practitioners, students, child minders and parents. The activities would be suitable for the development of motor skills in all children, irrespective of whether they have a 'diagnosis'.

What is Dyspraxia/Developmental Co-ordination Disorder (DCD)?

The appearance of motor co-ordination difficulties in children is not a new problem. However, it has only relatively recently become more well known. Even 15 years ago terms like Dyspraxia (inefficiencies in formulating motor plans) was little heard of in the UK. In the past, the child presenting with motor co-ordination difficulties would have been considered 'clumsy' and possibly 'a bit slow'.

As the awareness has increased there has been a growing recognition that Dyspraxia is a specific learning difficulty (SpLD), rather than a generalised learning difficulty and is part of a spectrum of conditions including, Dyslexia, ADHD (Attention Deficit Hyperactivity Disorder) and Asperger's Syndrome. Studies in the area also suggest that there is an overlap between these types of conditions, where a child can have a mixture of difficulties rather than a single specific difficulty.

Over the years many terms have been used to describe this group of children. These terms include 'minimal brain dysfunction', 'clumsy child syndrome' and 'motor learning difficulties'. Some terms have been subsequently discarded as they have unfavourable connotations.

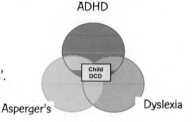

The problem is, the more we learn about the condition the more professionals have to revise their thinking, and this has led to a difficulty in ensuring consistent use of the term this group of children. Although there is a variety of terms used in books and resources, the term Dyspraxia is still very much in use.

However, the term Developmental Co-ordination Disorder is now becoming standard and will be used throughout this book to describe children with motor co-ordination difficulties.

5

Developmental Co-ordination Disorder affects between five and seven percent of the population, and boys appear to be affected more frequently and more severely than girls. This means that there may be at least one child with this disorder in a nursery setting at any one time. The condition results in difficulty with controlling and co-ordinating movement, despite normal intelligence and a lack of damage to muscles or nerves.

A diagnosis should only be reached following a period of observation within the nursery/school setting, and a full assessment by a pediatrician and/or an occupational therapist/physiotherapist

What causes/ Developmental Co-ordination Disorder?

The causes of DCD remain unclear. Many studies suggest that it is a disorder resulting from an immaturity in the developing brain. However, what is now becoming evident is that both environmental and genetic factors may have an influence.

DCD is also referred to as a multi-factorial condition i.e. there are likely to be several different causes for children presenting with these same complex symptoms. DCD s not a disease, but a group of symptoms that together make up the diagnosis. For some children there will be a clear family history. DCD cannot be 'caught' and there are not 'blood tests' for diagnosis. There is as yet no cure.

The term developmental means that DCD is not just a disorder of childhood. The nature of the condition often changes as the child grows up. The things that a child may find hard to do when he is five years old, such as riding a trike, kicking a ball or putting on shoes are usually mastered by the time he is around ten. By the time the child is an adult, they may not need to use these skills at all. It therefore can appear that the child grows out of the condition. However, up to 50% of the more severely affected children continue to have difficulties as adults.

It is important to point out that several of the distinguishing features of DCD are also observable in some general medical conditions. If DCD is suspected it is important to establish the underlying cause for the concern as early as possible.

The following medical conditions can mimic DCD:

? Cerebral Palsy (CP);

? Motor co-ordination difficulties associated with head injury (such as that incurred through a road traffic accident);

? Generalised developmental delay (GDD);

? Progressive muscular diseases such as Muscular Dystrophy;

? Motor co-ordination difficulties which may be part of other specific developmental disorders e.g. Attention Deficit and Hyperactivity Disorder (ADHD), Asperger's Syndrome (AS).

However, what is known is that DCD is not a disease and it cannot be transmitted, neither is it life threatening. There are no blood tests for it like those for arthritis, heart disease and diabetes. It cannot be cured; neither surgery nor drugs have anything to offer.

Issues Around Early Identification

DCD in its milder form is harder to identify in the early years due to the range normal child development.

Often the child achieves motor milestones within normal limits, and their ability may seem to be reasonably consistent with their peers. Any gap may not be that

great, and expectations at this age may not be so high. As the child is more likely to be male, it is often assumed that any delay in his mastery of motor skills are due to his gender, as it is generally accepted that boys develop at a slower rate than girls at this stage. Delay may be greeted with such opinions as 'Well he's a boy, and he'll soon grow out of it'.

The Characteristics of DCD

A number of the following features may be apparent, but each child is different and no one child presents the same as another.

Gross Motor Skills

- Late motor milestones - the child may have been later sitting, crawling, walking or talking. Some children may not have crawled at all, although around ten percent of all children can miss out this stage of motor development.
- Balance problems - the child may be unreasonably afraid, or conversely unaware of danger in precarious situations. Climbing on a climbing frame or along a wall, or walking downstairs may make the child very nervous. The child may also be unstable when sitting on a chair, especially if their feet are not firmly on the floor. The child can often be seen 'hanging on' to the seat of the table with their hands.
- Running - may be ungainly. Stopping with any control may be very hard to do, with the child often crashing into things as a result.
- Large play - the child may actively avoid climbing on play equipment or find it harder to pedal trikes and bikes.
- High levels of motor activity - the child is constantly on the go or seems weak and easily tired.
- Accident prone - the child has lots of little accidents such as spilling milk, or big accidents such as falling off play equipment or trikes/bikes, or unintentionally knocking into other children.
- Complaints more about minor physical injuries. Bumps and bruises bother children with DCD more than other children.
- Dislikes rough play.
- Feels floppy, like a 'rag doll' when picked up

Fine Motor Skills

- Grasps and grips - they may have difficulty holding and manipulating small objects e.g. doing up buttons, holding and using a pencil, using scissors, and playing with small construction toy.
- Hand preference - this may be very late being established. Difficulty may be experienced when using two hands together for activities such as threading.
- Tool control - the child may have poorer pencil control from making marks, patterns and shapes. They may have difficulty holding and using scissors to snip or cut. Managing holding and using a spoon or fork may be more difficult picture of child attempting to draw.
- May frequently break toys unintentionally.

Learning Skills

There may be difficulties with:

- recognising shapes;
- simple numbers - counting and recognising numbers;
- simple puzzles and construction activities.

Language and Communication Skills

Difficulties associated with:

- slower acquisition of speech;
- clarity of speech which may be even less distinct when the child is tired;
- social skills commensurate to age may be poorer;
- difficulty following instructions appropriate to the child's age;
- lack of imaginative play.

Social and Emotional development

There may be difficulties with:

- concentration compared to peers;
- emotional sensitivity to things that happen, feeling easily hurt, inability tolerate upsets and may become agitated when routines are changed unexpectedly;
- insecurity - particularly when separating from parent/carer;
- high levels of excitability;
- sensitivity to sensory stimuli;
- avoids certain types of play - construction play or pencil/crayon tasks and other activities needing fine motor control.

Self Care Skills

- Feeding and drinking - Persistent feeding difficulties, intolerance to certain foods, restricted diet;
- Evidence of sleeping difficulties - poor bedtime routines and sleep patterns, constant waking and needing reassurance;
- Little interest in dressing themselves, or may be delayed in developing age appropriate aspects of dressing. May be a very messy eater, preferring to use fingers rather than a fork or a spoon;
- Toilet training may be delayed.

Why is Movement so Important?

Motor development influences intellectual, social and emotional development. Exploration leads to knowledge and understanding about the world and how we fit into it. It also helps us to develop and formulate concepts and ideas which later are shown through drawing and writing. We learn to move and move to learn.

Why is it important to identify and support Children who may be a cause for Concern in the Foundation Phase?

When children reach primary level, greater demands are placed their co-ordination skills and the amount of time devoted to developing or consolidating these skills decreases. The more active the school curriculum becomes, the more some of the children with inefficient motor skills will have negative experiences in a greater range of school subjects.

At this stage most children begin to develop insight, but children with DCD may find it difficult to make sense of what is going on around them. Learning new skills is difficult and they do not know why. Behavioural manifestations such as temper tantrums and other inappropriate behaviour may become apparent.

In a more formal setting, the environment becomes more structured. Activities that could have escaped without notice in the park or in a playgroup setting now have to be confronted head on as they are integral to learning within a formal curriculum. Deficits in play skills become more evident. Studies have demonstrated that children with DCD were are likely to be vigorously active or play on large equipment. Studies also suggest that the DCD child tends to be more passive in play and more anxious than other children, and that children

who are 'clumsy' or socially inept are not well tolerated by their peers if they show any differences in expected playing styles. The longer term research suggests that adolescents and adults with DCD are at risk of developing socially deviant behaviours and mental health problems if the condition is not diagnosed and their needs met.

The early years practitioner therefore plays a very important role in the early identification of children with DCD and the Foundation Stage is a crucial time for children with motor co-ordination difficulties to consolidate skills before the formal curriculum makes too many demands on them.

Characteristics of Children with DCD in the Early Years Setting

Recognising and understanding these may help practitioners to be aware of the play and learning opportunities to offer when working with younger children. Such early knowledge and intervention may help in preventing or reducing the impact of DCD on the developing child who may have:

* poor organisation skills - self management and work;
* difficulties in PE and games - gymnastics, games and dance;
* problems with personal care, such as dressing;
* literacy difficulties - in spelling, writing, pencil control;
* limited attention and concentration;
* some difficulty in both making and maintaining friendships;
* problems in following and interpreting verbal information;
* low self confidence and self esteem;
* numeracy difficulties - in areas like mental maths, presentation and layout, 3D shape, rotation/symmetry;
* problems when managing tools or apparatus in science, maths, design, technology;
* verbal skills which are often better than performance skills;
* some times see things literally which can be misinterpreted as being cheeky;
* avoidance behaviours which are misinterpreted as inattention or disobedience.

Other factors to consider which may impact on the child's development of motor skills:

It is vital to remember that other factors **may** affect a child's development, here are some:

- ✓ chronological age and birth month;
- ✓ body build - some children are naturally tall or larger framed and this may influence their choice of activities and quality of movements. Overweight children may find the more physical activities uncomfortable, and the their size may restrict them in what they can or want to play with;
- ✓ maturation;
- ✓ family position;
- ✓ first language;
- ✓ intellectual competence;
- ✓ environment/social setting;
- ✓ experience and opportunity to practice;
- ✓ temperament.

Observation is the Key to successful identification of needs

Why do we need to observe and assess?

? To understand underlying needs

? To provide structure for resources and strategies for skills development

? To point the direction towards appropriate support or referral if necessary

When observing children playing it is easy to see a range of competence. There are those who move with competence and confidence, those who can do it but not very well - their movements appearing awkward and ungainly compared with other children. These children may not persevere with a task, and if they do their skills do not appear to improve. They may not appear to enjoy the activity and quickly learn to avoid activities that challenge them.

Here are some aspects to consider when observing children at play:

✋ How is the child moving? - slow/fast, deliberate?

     Can they sustain the movement?

     Are the movements fluid and rhythmical?

     Is the movement appropriate for the action - too strong, too fast?

     Can they make adjustments when the need is pointed out?

     Does the child have a sense of where their body is relative to others or equipment they are using?

✋ Where is the child moving?
>   Do they avoid certain activities such as playing on large apparatus?
>   Do they avoid playing near other children?
>   Do they 'move' in the right direction?

Often it is the quality of the child's movement that draws your attention. Using a set of abilities criteria is often helpful in describing the child's skills, and indicates the type of help and support they may need to become successful. These simple criteria can be used when making judgements about what you observe and in planning next steps for groups and individuals:

- ☞ **Not Close** - Child finds it impossible even with support;
- ☞ **Almost** - Manages independently but with great difficulty;
- ☞ **Just** - Manages independently with some effort;
- ☞ **Well** - No real difficulty.

Some Questions to Consider if you are Concerned

?   Is the child's movement delayed in all aspects or just in specific areas relating to co-ordination?

?   What is the pace of the child's development? Is it within the normal range, or deviating?

?   Are you aware of any specific learning difficulties in the family e.g. older siblings that you may have known? Have you talked to the child's parents?

?   Do you know if the child was late in reaching any of his developmental milestones? Have you talked to the child's parents?

?   Are there signs of frustration or anger?

While it is possible to describe some of the features of DCD that may present in younger children, it is important to point out that not all children who bump into things or fall over a lot should be considered as having DCD.

Practitioners should be aware that if a child displays a cluster of these characteristics they should be observed over a period of time, across a range of activities. Some intervention should be instigated in order to ascertain if progress is made. While early identification is useful, it is important not to label the child and potentially alarm and distress the parents. Onward referral to appropriate agencies should be the first step.

Motor Skills Checklists for the Foundation Stage Practitioner

1. Gross Motor Skills

Abilities	Date	Date	Date	Action
Can run skillfully around obstacles and corners also while pushing/pulling large toys				**Strategies and resources**
Can throw a ball and catch a large ball with arms outstretched				
Can kick a ball with some force				
Can ride a tricycle with skill and make sharp turns easily				
Can use a variety of play equipment including slides, swings and climbing frames with agility				
Can judge body space in play eg fitting into confined spaces or negotiating holes and boundaries				
Can demonstrate the control necessary to hold a shape or fixed position				
Can walk along a low beam (10cm wide) for a short distance				**Further action/Referral**
Can persevere in repeating actions or attempts when developing a new skill				**Strategies and resources**
Exhibits some appropriate awareness of safety measures				
Engages in organised play which has some rules				
Can sustain physical play (endurance and stamina) appropriate to age				

14

Motor Skills Checklists for the Foundation Stage Practitioner

2. Fine Motor Skills

Abilities	Date	Date	Date	Action
Can control a pencil using thumb and first two fingers near the point to draw a developmentally appropriate image of a person				**Strategies and resources**
Can copy simple shapes onto large paper with crayon or pencil				
Can cut with scissors continuously straight within ? inch guideline				
Can thread beads onto a lace				
Can use cutlery (spoon/fork/knife)				
Can make simple objects combining play material - design evident				
Can use tools to make things				
Can insert small objects into holes such as peg boards/sorters/containers				**Further action/Referral**
Can fasten large front buttons				**Strategies and resources**
Can manipulate toys which unscrew and screw				
Can roll, squeeze, manipulate playdough to form simple shapes				
Can pour flowing substances from one container to another				

Behaviour and DCD

The child with DCD may display negative or disruptive behaviour, not because he/she is trying to gain attention but rather because their difficulties impose constraints on their ability to concentrate and carry out tasks, and this has a knock-on effect on behaviour. Having to concentrate, balance, listen, think and do is too much, and creates overload for the child. This becomes evident in words, actions or both words and actions.

Often our first response when we see a child repeating the same negative behaviour is that the child is being naughty, rather than considering that this is a way of telling us he is finding it harder to do something than other children may.

As well as observing motor skills, take time to reflect upon the ABC's of behaviour:

A = antecedents - what happened before

B = the behaviour and

C = what was the consequence if the child has frequent tantrums.

Working with Parents of Children with DCD

Because of the nature of DCD, an early diagnosis is quite unusual. Some parents may not be aware there is a problem, it is you that is concerned. Take care how you approach a discussion, so you don't alarm parents unnecessarily.

Some parents may become increasingly concerned about their child, knowing something is 'not quite right' yet not knowing what it is. They may be seeing differences in their child's abilities compared with other children. They may

have been chatting to other parents at the school gate. While it is tempting to dismiss concerns raised by parents, suggesting to parents that their the child is 'doing OK', it is important to monitor and document areas of concern, reassure parents and keep them fully informed.

Parents may come to you expressing any (or many) of the following feelings:

☞ **Frustration** - 'I don't understand what is wrong. 'If only he/she would try harder', 'I don't know where to turn for help, nobody seems to want to help me'.

☞ **Anger** - 'Why me? Why don't my friends have the same problems as we have?' 'I feel angry with my partner/husband/wife; he/she doesn't seem to understand what I have to go through, having a child with all sorts of difficulties and trying to cope with the rest of the family? Everyone thinks I am just making it up.'

☞ **Guilt** - 'Is it my fault? Maybe I didn't eat properly during the pregnancy; maybe the delivery was too fast or too slow. Perhaps it is something in my genes. Sometimes I shout at my son, and afterwards I feel like I shouldn't have, but I just can't see why he can't do some of the simplest things.'

☞ **Isolation** - 'We feel like the only people in the world with a child who has these problems. Nobody else seems to understand. My child looks normal, but I know he is different. I wish I could talk to someone about it.'

☞ **Relief** - Being given an explanation or reassurance that there is help can be a relief for many parents. Just having a name for the problem can help parents understand and explain to others why their child is having difficulties.

☞ **Acceptance** - This can often be difficult for parents and some feel the need to constantly seek service agencies, looking for answers.

☞ **Ability to cope** - The family has to deal with all sorts of information and advice. This can be overwhelming and the parents may feel the future is bleak and don't know where to start. This can cause friction between parents, and with siblings. Parents may feel that they are in constant battle with the school system in an attempt to get the right sort of help for their child.

Francine Bates; Chief Executive of Contact a Family offers these top tips for practitioners from parents:

✓ Welcome me and my child
✓ Give me useful information
✓ Remember I am very busy
(we forget that bringing up a child with additional needs is VERY hard work!)
✓ Don't patronise me or feel sorry for me
✓ Don't tell me my child is a problem
✓ Help me find solutions

So what can practitioners do to support parents?

- Give them time to talk.
- Be prepared to listen.
- Provide information that they can take away, and an opportunity to come back and ask further questions.
- Be honest about what you are seeing with the child but try not to give predictions for the future. Every child is different despite having an identified difficulty with a name.
- Explain what is happening - keep them up to date.
- Work together - helping parents to maintain the links between agencies and services. The family of a child with complex difficulties may be involved with multiple agencies.
- Understand and keep up to date yourself about developments and research into DCD and similar difficulties
- Put together a resource box, so parents can have some ideas of activities they can do at home.
- Keep a directory of local resources and agencies.

Supporting the Learning of Children with DCD
Adapting the setting and the task

Children need to learn through their own efforts and in their own way. Once they learn to do this they can interact with their environment with enthusiasm and enjoyment. Children with DCD may need to be encouraged to take initiative and responsibility for their own learning and experiences. You may need to help this by modifying the environment in ways that work for them.

Modifications should not be seen as external - designed by the adult for the child. If the child is going to become independent (and to develop self-esteem and confidence) they must encounter the world as it is and learn strategies to solve problems as they encounter them. Children should have a say; you must involve them in the conversation!

When considering adaptations to your learning environment, consider:

? Have the wishes, thoughts and and desires of the child been taken into consideration?
? Does this adaptation say to the child 'You are not able' or 'You can'?
? How will it benefit the child?
? Is it developmentally appropriate?
? Is it the least intrusive way of meeting the child's needs?
? Does it preserve the dignity of the child?
? What does the adaptation say to other children? How have they been involved and informed?
? Does this adaptation blend into the natural environment of your setting?

Let the children have their say

Remember - it will be more effective and enjoyable if you involve the child in the discussion.

Here are some ways practitioners adapt the learning environment:

! They alter or change the resources/equipment being used;
! They eliminate a stage of the activity;
! They reduce the group size for the activity - groups to pairs/pairs to individual;
! They change the teaching and learning style - practical or verbal instead of written, active instead of passive, individual instead of group
! They change the environment - the way the room is set up, access to equipment, space, organisation of the day etc.

Activities should be enjoyable, and consistency is a key word. Children should be given sufficient time, short sequences should be practiced over a variety of activities and challenges.

Environmental considerations

No matter how enriching an environment is, it is not enriching for the child who cannot access it!

Sometimes the desire to 'fix' the child by improving their skills overshadows the importance of making changes to the environment. Without these changes, the child's motivation and opportunities to become engaged in play and learning will be diminished.

Risk plays an important role in learning

Physical structure ▯ the way space is organised.

This should be consistent with the the national guidance on learning activities and curricular goals. It should also allow children to remain engaged in meaningful learning activities. The balance between requirements and the needs of the child is sometimes difficult to maintain!

Safety reduces accidents but it can foster feelings of security by removing 'safe risks'. Children are more likely to explore their environment if they feel safe, but at times we create environments that are devoid of risks. This limits the child's exposure to new experiences, and children need these to stimulate exploration and at times learn from their mistakes. Risk-taking plays an important role in learning new skills, so we must be able to make informed decisions about the difference between a safe risk and an unacceptable danger.

- ✓ Use photos of individual children to mark their personal possessions;
- ✓ Ensure the equipment is sturdy and well maintained;
- ✓ Minimise clutter;
- ✓ Ensure routes from one area to another are direct. Minimise cross traffic. Use visual reinforcement e.g. - Cut out foot prints to follow from one area to another;
- ✓ Prosthetize - attach additional parts for easier access e.g. knobs on wooden puzzles or rulers;
- ✓ Stabilise activities - use sturdy surfaces or non-slip matting such as Dycem (see resources);
- ✓ Avoid isolating the child;
- ✓ Seat the child away from distractions;
- ✓ Present materials on contrasting backgrounds;
- ✓ Ensure adequate lighting;
- ✓ Use Backward Chaining - this is where the last element of a task is taught first. When that has been mastered the last but one and last component is taught, an so on, until the task has been taught from the end to the start instead of the start to the finish;

Consistency and enjoyment are the keys to learning

✓ Pictures on drawers of objects with photo of child;
✓ Footprints on the floor.

Promote interaction with the environment

Some children with DCD fail to become engaged
in an activity unless there is some guidance from
you:

- 👋 Encourage them to practise making choices
  and taking turns at every opportunity.
- 👋 Use modelling, prompting, or physical
  assistance.
- 👋 Children may also need help to stay or play
  with an activity over time - play beside, responding to or commenting on
  their play. Assist them when needed, but don't be too quick to do it for
  them!
- 👋 Provide appealing material - colour, size, sound, texture. 3 dimensional
  objects are more appealing than 2 dimensional ones. Create novelty and
  feedback for the child.
- 👋 Make the tasks more familiar - use objects or symbols that represent the
  child's world and interests
- 👋 Reduce the required response - minimise the distance for attention.

Promote social interaction

Think carefully about the activities you present - some promote or foster particular behaviours. Group size can also influence interaction. A non-competitive
teaching strategy promotes:

- 👋 asking for help or offering help;
- 👋 listening to others;
- 👋 sharing materials and ideas;
- 👋 turn taking;
- 👋 showing someone;
- 👋 helping someone to accomplish
  a task.

Promote independence

It is essential to get the balance between fostering independence - persuading children to do things on their own - and ensuring that they are not left out of activities because they lack the required skills. It is important that adults avoid over-controlling the environment for children with any additional needs.

- Make participation a privilege not a duty.
- Give children immediate roles within each activity.
- Identify children's preferences for materials and equipment.
- Establish and maintain a daily routine.
- Allow a reluctant child to observe a group until they are ready to join in.

Children who cannot control their environment often develop 'learned helplessness'.

- Be aware of the child's developmental level.
- Give time for generalisation across a variety of setting and activities.
- Always ensure success. Continued failure and isolation from their peers in games and play can reinforce feelings of inadequacy and the child can become isolated and withdrawn. Refusal to participate may result. This is often misinterpreted as 'bad behaviour' but it may be a reluctance to set themselves up to fail.

Try not to over-control the environment for children with any sort of additional need

- It may be necessary for you to model the behaviour. Use the following if the child has difficulty:
  - ☐ gently hold their arm and move it to help imitate the actions;
  - ☐ gradually reduce your physical involvement as the child becomes more confident and competent;
  - ☐ finally carry out the activity alongside them.
- Reward the child with praise when they complete a task or game. If they are reluctant, don't coax or bribe them. Let them see that you are enjoying it, and this will encourage them to participate.
- If the child is bored with a toy, try presenting it in different ways such as hiding it in a 'feely' bag or box.
- Encourage the child to talk about what they are doing as they do it.

Provide children with predictable and immediate feedback

An environment which ensures this helps children to acquire a sense of power and security in controlling their environment. It can also be highly motivating and encourages children to maintain concentration over time. Children who feel they have no control over their environment often develop 'learned helplessness'. Some ways to vary the activities:

- 🖐 Output or performance - adapt how you want the child to respond to an instructional task.
- 🖐 Type of participation - adapt the amount of active involvement the child can have in the task.
- 🖐 Expand your presentation and delivery of materials - provide more hands on experiences.
- 🖐 Provide frequent visual cues to reinforce understanding.
- 🖐 Use specific terminology.
- 🖐 Repeat and expand on what the child says.
- 🖐 Keep directions and instructions short and simple.
- 🖐 Model the correct language usage.
- 🖐 Speak clearly and face the child when talking to them.

> **Keep instructions short and simple, provide visual clues, give them time to respond.**

- 🖐 Be alert for subtle responses which indicate that a child is learning and communicating e.g. breathing, eye or head movements
- 🖐 Provide frequent positive feedback.
- 🖐 Allow time for learning, practice, repetition and completion of tasks.
- 🖐 Introduce calming activities after vigorous play.

23

Strategies for
Supporting Children
with DCD
PERSONAL, SOCIAL
AND EMOTIONAL
DEVELOPMENT

Ideas and activities to try

✓ Offer activities which stimulate all the senses.
✓ Use positioning for activities which does not distract the child from the task - provide appropriate seating and comfort/postural support, such as allowing the child to lie down to listen instead of sitting.
✓ Encourage the development of personal space - their own coat hook, work tray etc.
✓ Have structure and support for transition of activities:
   * provide simple rules;
   * be consistent;
   * plan and prepare for changes in events and situations by using stories, video, visitors, visual timetables.
✓ Plan activities which develop social and practical language skills (body language/facial expression) such as:
   * role play, puppets and dolls;
   * role modelling;
   * playing turn-taking games and activities;
   * encouraging and modelling self help skills;
   * helping with chores/errands.

✓ Encourage negotiating and bargaining skills.
✓ Help the child to verbalise opinions and desires.
✓ Use stories and role play to explore roles of others - police, nurses etc.
✓ Use large play equipment to develop a sense of safety for self and others.
✓ Plan simple co-operative games and turn-taking.
✓ Develop problem-solving skills such as choice-making, sequencing and organisation through hands-on investigations, encouraging suggestions and solutions.
✓ Promote independent self-care activities by:
   * establishing everyday routines and tasks;
   * adapting activities as appropriate to ensure success eg Velcro, larger buttons, clothes without fastenings;
   * pretend play and dressing up;
   * doll dressing activities, button books, lacing cards;
   * sequencing puzzles, specially of familiar events.

- ✓ Promote the recognition of dangerous situations and taking of action to protect oneself.
- ✓ Have access to methods of expressing thoughts and feelings:
  - * smiley faces;
  - * feelings cards;
  - * expression games.
- ✓ Provide experiences and activities which have boundaries and limitations, both in child directed play and adult directed activities:
  - * simple board games;
  - * physical games;
  - * ICT programs.
- ✓ Offer rules and boundaries which are explained in a way the child can understand. These could be:
  - * verbal,
  - * pictorial,
  - * gesture,
  - * demonstration.

Strategies for Supporting Children with DCD MATHEMATICAL DEVELOPMENT

Ideas and activities to try

- ✓ Use outdoor and physical play to develop concepts of the shape and size of the child's own body and how it relates to space around them:
- ✓ Play rhythm games e.g. clapping, tapping.
- ✓ Reinforce rhythm through poems and rhymes (in music sessions).
- ✓ Plan problem solving through play and routine activities:
  - * what if?
  - * how can I / you?
  - * is there another way?
- ✓ Develop concepts of order and sequencing in every day routine activities and play:
  - * lining up items,
  - * organising themselves in tasks 'first we need to'.

- ✓ Participating in singing, music and movement sessions.
- ✓ Play finger games and rhymes e.g. 'Two Little Dicky Birds', 'Five Fat Sausages'.
- ✓ Continue to work with more complex shape sorters and puzzle activities.

- ✓ Support the development of concepts of direction and position:
    - * relating self to object (stand behind the chair; sit on the red cushion);
    - * relating object to object (put the brick under the bucket, throw the ball into the box).
- ✓ Use bricks, blocks and shapes, dominoes, pentominoes, interlocking shapes, construction sets.
- ✓ Use mirrors in play. Play mirror games in physical activities.
- ✓ Offer activities which require pouring and filling containers.
- ✓ Plan activities using scales, measuring sticks, tapes, trundle wheels in:

    - * sand and messy play;
    - * simple cooking;
    - * construction;
    - * creative work.
- ✓ Include table top games and art and craft activities which promote concepts of pattern:
    - * pegs, lacing, mosaic tiles;
    - * pre- writing activities, such as printing stampers, rollers;
    - * posting boxes.
- ✓ Reinforce language through every day activities for shape concepts.
- ✓ Play specifically directed games and activities which focus on space, shape and position, such as:
    - * shape walks;
    - * using feely bags;
    - * hide and find with shapes;
    - * using large equipment to go 'through', 'over', 'under', climbing 'up', 'down', 'on top', 'on the bottom';
    - * pulling and pushing objects around their environment

        - * play singing games which have a prepositional context 'Farmer's in his Den', 'In and Out the Dusty Bluebells';
        - * sing lots of action rhymes and jingles
        - * use stories with clear sequences and story lines;
        - * use positional language in routine tasks such as tidying up - 'Put the dolls in the box', 'Put this box under the shelf'.

Strategies for Supporting Children with DCD

COMMUNICATION, LANGUAGE AND LITERACY

✓ Don't overload conversation, keep it simple.
✓ Avoid 'cross examining' - take care with questions when children find it difficult to talk.
✓ Avoid correcting. Instead, re-state what the child is trying to say, going for the meaning rather than correcting the language.
✓ Use turn-taking activities
✓ Gently extend the child's utterances (but resist the temptation to finish their sentences for them!)and reflect back what the child has said back to them
  * check for hearing problems if concerns arise
  * be patient when the child is trying to communicate
✓ Develop their listening skills by:
  * checking the environment - position, visual distractions, auditory distractions, level of the task - can they hear you?
  * checking whether the child has the developmental skill level you are expecting;
  * combining auditory and visual channels - decrease the environmental distractions when they are working, and increase number of children/adults present, so they don't feel exposed;
  * clarifying and extending their understanding of boundaries in play and routine activities - make sure they understand simple instructions such as 'Come here', 'Sit on this chair', 'Look at my face';
  * repeating and chunking information, backing it up with visual cues.

COMMUNICATION, LANGUAGE AND LITERACY (Continued)

- ✓ Play games which promote sequencing and 'What happens next?':
  - * sequencing toys and cards;
  - * stories;
  - * TV or video programmes.
- ✓ Share the roles in conversation - being the listener AND communicator.
- ✓ Develop your skills in being able to use 'repair' strategies when communication breaks down - be honest, listen to their reasons, go slowly and be prepared to repeat a step or go back to a previous stage.
- ✓ Make sure you have the child's attention BEFORE you start communicating.
- ✓ Monitor signs of comprehension.
- ✓ Practice ways of defining and using words in other Foundation Stage activities in Maths, Knowledge and Understanding of the World, Creativity.

Strategies for Supporting Children with DCD KNOWLEDGE AND UNDERSTANDING OF THE WORLD

- ✓ Offer construction activities such as 'Lego', 'Duplo', 'Stickle Bricks', 'Playmobil'.
- ✓ Give plenty of experience with water play (tipping and pouring into containers), using tubes, funnels, bottles, containers of a range of types and sizes to help with control and co-ordination through play.
- ✓ Develop fine motor skills by planning activities for handling and using a variety of tools for construction such as:
  - * scissors;
  - * hammer, saws, screwdrivers;
  - * hole punches, staplers, tape dispensers;
  - * spreaders, brushes and mark makers;
  - * cooking equipment such as whisks, forks, knives and spreaders.
- ✓ Use sand play, with toys and objects which require a range of fine motor skills - sieves, funnels, rollers, trucks and other vehicles.
- ✓ Toys that involve rotation - turning knobs, poking buttons through holes, turning keys etc.
- ✓ Play with a range of different sized bricks and blocks - building, balancing, stacking etc.
- ✓ For children with severe difficulties, try magnetic or Velcro blocks to ensure success and a sense of achievement.

Some children with DCD dislike messy activities and textured materials. In extreme cases, a particular texture can even cause a child to vomit. Make sure you ask parents about their child's extreme like and dislikes and take these into account when planning activities. Introduce them slowly and carefully, and note the child's reactions.

Encourage children to participate in:

✓ construction activities, working with both large and small equipment;

✓ singing activities, rhymes and action songs;

✓ playing simple musical instruments;

✓ novel and stimulating activities that encourage the use of all the senses.

Use activities which spontaneously produce a mark with little effort:

✓ magic painting books;

✓ candle painting - rub a candle over paper then paint over to reveal the marks;

✓ etching and rubbings;

✓ carbon paper between leaves of drawing paper; scribble or write, then reveal what's underneath.

CREATIVE DEVELOPMENT (Continued)

Continue to develop experiences of manipulating and using construction activities, navigation and negotiation of space, perceptual activities and sensory activities using:

- ✓ natural colours and shapes in living things;
- ✓ more complex puzzles and problem solving activities involving shape;
- ✓ extended experiences with textures and materials;
- ✓ children's own bodies to develop concepts of space.

Develop tactile skills:

- ✓ through construction activities and other fine motor toys;
- ✓ by offering a variety of textured media - grading from hard to soft and dry to wet (sand play, water play, messy play);
- ✓ by playing 'Guess what's in the bag?';
- ✓ by using hands as templates for patterns to draw around or draw on, using body paints;
- ✓ getting used to handling and using different textured materials - cotton wool, feathers, crepe paper, food stuff such as potato printing;
- ✓ playing finger songs and rhymes.

Strategies for Supporting Children with DCD and Physical Development

This is obviously the major area for support. Some children may dislike activities which require their feet to be off the ground, or the use of rotation movements such as roundabouts, or linear movements such as swings and slides. Introduction of this type of activity will need careful handling.

✓ Use a range of play equipment which encourages the use of sensory motor skills:
* climbing frames, swings and spinning apparatus;
* tunnels, soft play;
* ball pools;
* water - paddling pools and water tray play;
* textured walks - use carpet tiles, fur fabric, sand and bubble wrap;
* feely bags/hide and seek objects in different substances;
* log roll along bubble paper, corrugated cardboard or a half pumped air mattress/lilo.

✓ Practice the development of motor control in graduating movements by planning activities which encourage the child to:
* stop when rolling;
* stop when crawling (commando to all fours);
* stop when walking;
* stop when trotting/galloping;
* stop when running.

✓ Promote the development of knowledge and understanding of body parts
* in 'Simple Simon' games;
* in ring games such as 'Okey Kokey';
* in action to instruction games such as 'Put your finger on your nose'.

✓ Use large play equipment, exploring getting the body 'in', 'onto', 'through' 'under'.

✓ Use large play equipment such as trikes and carts, driving them around the setting and around obstacles.

✓ Develop sufficient body and arm strength through:
  * weight bearing activities such as crawling on all fours;
  * propping on arms (lie on tummy propped on arms to listen to a story);
  * rough and tumble play;
  * activities which require using arms away from the body - 'whizzers/speed balls', ribbons on sticks.

✓ Use push and pull along toys/equipment.

✓ Develop visual motor co-ordination and integration (eye/hand co-ordination), practising gross motor activities first, then moving onto fine motor skills:
  * ball games - roll ball to hit an object (skittles);
  * play games which involve rolling the ball to and from the child;
  * Etch a Sketch;
  * paper and pencil mazes and dot to dots;
  * threading games;
  * bead mazes;
  * painting and construction.

✓ When introducing scissor skills, work through a developmental progression such as this, to ensure success:
  * snip at the edges of paper;
  * snip across 1" strips;
  * cut across the width of A4 paper;
  * introduce single lines which change direction;
  * cut out simple straight lined shapes (circles should be last);
  * remember - card is easier to manage than thin paper.

✓ Offer creative activities in art and craft, which require the use of equipment like rollers, stampers and scissors.

✓ Encourage pretend play activities:
  * screwdrivers and spanners in construction sets;
  * saucepans, kettles, wooden spoons, whisks, cutlery, hoovers, irons etc in pretend play to develop wrist and finger skills.

✓ Develop the co-ordination and control of limbs <u>and</u> body with full body movement such as:

  * reaching up tall - stretching arms to the sky, standing on tip toes
  * curling up into a ball
  * reaching arms and legs out to the sides
  * twisting their body while keeping their legs still
  * balancing - holding a variety of positions, working from lying on their back, tummy, side, low kneeling, high kneeling then standing
  * balancing on equipment e.g. on a low bench
  * balancing while moving - climbing or walking on equipment

✓ Provide activities which are challenging and stimulating and promote differing levels of movement patterns including the ability to:
  * sustain weight through their arms and travelling using hands and feet, such as crawling or walking on all fours
  * differentiate movement patterns such as marching;
  * differential movement patterns - right from left such as skipping and hopping
  * differentiate movement patterns - bottom left /top right; bottom right/top left, such as commando crawling
  * rotate around their central body axis, such as log rolling
  * shift their body weight and adjust their stance to balance when their body is working outside the centre of balance, such as stepping over low hurdles, or on/off low obstacles.

- ✓ Link movements to feelings, such as 'Jump for joy' 'Run away!' 'Jump!' 'Scary stuff, hide your eyes!' 'Happy dance'.

- ✓ Practice movement skills which involve navigating and negotiating space.

- ✓ Participate in activities which promote reciprocal stepping, such as:
  - * stepping up and onto/over and down from low surfaces
  - * stepping over a sequence of low obstacles
  - * Provide physical support for balance and security to help the child maintain sequences of movement.

- ✓ Develop and use self-correction, by constructively drawing attention to actions.

- ✓ Encourage the expression of ideas, suggestions and solutions

- ✓ Plan collaborative and co-operative games.

- ✓ Ensure hand preference is established, by systematically working through activities which promote:
  - * Symmetrical hand use - activities which require the same actions to be carried out with both hands, such as throwing a ball with 2 hands, using a rolling pin to roll out dough;
  - * Asymmetrical tasks where one hand 'does' and the other 'helps', such as threading, stirring mixtures, screw toys, cutting.

- ✓ Develop control over objects by playing games which encourage:

  - * Reaching and touching/grasping objects which are stationary - reach for named toys/objects placed in front or around the child e.g. 'Show me the blue one'
  - * Reaching and touching objects which are moving slowly - horizontally, vertically, diagonally, unpredictably e.g. popping bubbles by poking using the index finger

✓ Develop co-ordination skills, starting with the child reaching and grasping with both hands together when catching a ball; then encourage using their preferred hand alone, then their non-preferred hand alone. Work from playing with large objects to small objects

✓ Encourage eye control by:
   * offering activities where the child must track and follow objects visually - travelling vertically, horizontally, diagonally and advancing towards them;
   * linking eye and hand movements - using slow moving objects such as balloons or inflatable balls which allow time for the child to prepare and respond with both hands;
   * use larger balls first and then gradually introduce smaller balls/objects.
   Check that the child is able to balance adequately to respond to the activity. Work from a sitting position before standing. Lying on their tummy to play ball games is also helpful for some children.

✓ Develop kicking and other ball skills in a sequence:
   * walk into the ball;
   * kick the ball from standing - with the ball still or held still by an adult;
   * kick a ball when rolled gently toward the child from a short distance (increase the distance over time and as skills progress);
   * use the feet to manoeuvre the ball.

Remember, this development may take some time and lots of practice!

✓ If the child cannot balance sufficiently to kick the ball:
  * play games that promote standing on one leg, such as stamping on bubbles;
  * let the child sit on a seat or chair to kick a ball placed in front of them;
  * use two broomsticks, one held in each hand to act as extra support. As balance improves encourage them to use one stick and progress to no sticks as competency and confidence is gained.

✓ Provide activities which promote the development of dexterity and manipulative skills. Plan activities and select toys which encourage:
  * isolation of index finger and thumb e.g. post pennies into a money box, placing pegs into a peg board and threading, pop-up toys, computer keyboards and mouse manipulation;
  * button pressing and knob turning;
  * malleable materials such as Play-Dough to develop hand strength.

✓ Use equipment within the local community to extend and vary physical activities and maintain interest in physical activities, which may be difficult and frustrating for some children with DCD - try:
  * parks;
  * soft play areas;
  * adventure playgrounds;
  * sports centres;
  * country parks;
  * city farms.

Developing Whole Body Motor Skills

Play is about learning through activity and fun

Play helps to develop the brain. Many people think of play as entertainment or 'fooling around'. However, for children, their play both before and after starting school is vital for their development and for future learning. Children who have not had a rich and stimulating environment do not make the links in their brains that support real learning.

A child who has limited interest in play and perhaps does not do the sorts of things that parents expect may give the impression that they are simply not interested. And of course, this may make parents avoid or remove certain activities or toys because 'They aren't interested in them.'

A child who is not interested in the whole range of early play activities may have a problem, and that problem may include a sensory processing difficulty. A child with motor co-ordination difficulties may have limited experiences, so they stick to simple and familiar toys, games and activities and end up with even less experience of the activities they find difficult. Some may also appear to be inflexible in play, disliking change and routine. This inflexibility and lack of confidence may make other children avoid playing with them.

Through play the child obtains sensory input from their body and from gravity that is essential for both motor and emotional development. The sensory input is what makes play fun. Running, turning, bending, touching things, pushing, pulling, rolling, crawling, climbing, jumping produce movement and touch sensations. One of the reasons children play is to get this input. They need lots of it while they are young and less when adults, although we never stop needing play however old we are! The more a child explores, the more their senses are stimulated and the more complex the response required. The more varied the play, the more it contributes to their development.

Play is also essential for developing the capacity to 'motor plan'. As they play, the child moves body parts in countless different ways, and the sensations from these movements add new sensory maps in their brains, their nervous systems and their muscles. Through large, full-body movements they learn to relate to the space around them. Through manipulation of small toys they learn to use their hands and fingers efficiently. Play expands competence and extends confidence.

Watch children closely when they are playing and think about the significance of what they are doing. It is all right if they get their hands dirty or their clothes stained with grass or dust. This is an inevitable part of learning as they push themselves to make more and more mature responses.

As you watch you may see children who become over-excited, frustrated, sad or hostile during play. Realise that these feelings may come from some failure in sensory motor processing. It may not be something that you have noticed before, it may be a motor setback for the child, which results in a behavioural response.

Such experiences can stop a child from learning. But if you can give them lots of emotional support without trying to control what they do, they will be motivated to try the task again and again until they master it.

Children also need to develop both sides of their bodies and both sides of their brains in order to learn the skills of writing, reading, balance and poise - all essential attributes of a competent learner. This means that all children need lots of experience of using both hands in activities, and children with DCD need them even more.

These activities include:
* using scissors;
* riding bikes and scooters;
* weaving and sewing;
* playing in sand, water, dough, clay, mud etc;
* playing percussion instruments;
* running, climbing and jumping.

Games to develop gross motor skills

Children need to develop strength, stamina and endurance as well as an awareness of their body and how it moves. Taking part in lots of gross motor play activities also helps to develop their ability to plan, organise and sequence a series of movements.

Obstacles: Create obstacle courses - crawling under/over duvets, blankets, pillows, behind chairs, under the table, through tunnels and tubes, up and down shallow steps, over small obstacles. Turn the game into an adventure story by collecting treasures or tokens en-route. Encourage the child to use their imagination, let them build their own course, planning and experimenting with different patterns and orders of obstacles.

Row the boat: Two children sit on the floor opposite each other, join hands and rock back and forth - trying to go as far as they can in each direction. Try to be rhythmical. They can sing 'Row, Row, Row the Boat...'. Speed can be increased by suggesting windy weather etc.

Tortoise: Make the child an imaginary backpack with a large bean bag, cushion or folded blanket and have them crawl between two points. Pretend to be a tortoise or a snail carrying their house on their back.

Walrus walk: Lying on their tummies with arms extended in front, children lift their upper body and walk using their arms, with the legs trailing behind (easier on smooth surfaces and with clothes on).

Hedgehogs: Curl into a tight ball with hands around knees and nose on knees. Keep the nose on the knees.

Hot Dogs: Lie on a gym mat, carpet sample or small duvet. The child pretends to be a sausage. Roll up the 'hot dog' in the mat then get the child to unroll themselves.

Donkey Derby: You will need mats or a carpeted area for this game. The children get down in an all fours crawling position and crawl as fast as possible down a pre-set course. Encourage the children to give themselves a name. Reward the winner, but don't forget the slow and steady!

Roly Poly: You will need a carpeted area or mats for this activity. The children lie on their backs with arms stretched above their heads. Trying to keep this position they log roll down a runway of mats or across the carpet.

Ribbon Writing: Attach a long piece of good quality ribbon to a small stick (or buy some ribbon sticks) and use them to make shapes and patterns in the air. Use language to reinforce letter formation and and direction. To make it harder draw simple shapes on to card. The child looks at the card and draws the shape in the air.

Walk the Shape: Make shapes with skipping ropes, broom handles, hoops etc. Encourage the child to move around the shape and encourage the language of the shape. Use other methods of movement around the shape such as log rolling, crawling, skipping etc.

Body Songs: There are many movement songs and ring games that can help children with gross motor development. Here are a few: 'Heads, Shoulders, Knees and Toes'; 'In and out the Dusty Bluebells', 'Put your Finger in the Air', 'Duck, Duck, Goose', 'Wind the Bobbin up'; 'Here we go Round the Mulberry Bush'.

Parachute Games

Chute-ball: Best played with a large ball. Place the ball in the middle of the chute and by all pulling upwards and outwards, throw the ball as high in the air as possible.

Popcorn: Start with all the children holding the chute stretched out. Throw as many balls or balloons as you can find on top of the chute, then see how quickly you can throw them all off without letting go of the edge of the chute, of course. Alternatively, have half the children trying to keep them on the chute while the other half try to throw them off.

For recuperation after an energetic game, hold the chute stretched out and have about a third of the children lie in the group under it (best with heads near the middle). The rest mushroom the chute up and quickly pull it down again repeatedly. Air rushing in and out cools those underneath like a giant fan, and the sensation of watching the chute rise up and come down on top of you is very strange. Change round so everyone has a turn underneath.

Get a large piece of Lycra or knitted material and use this for pulling, stretching and waving activities - you don't need to buy a parachute!

More details of suppliers and books on page 57/58.

Developing Fine Motor Skills

Fine motor control is the ability to use the hands and fingers precisely for skilled activities, and involves hand/eye co-ordination.

Fine motor skills develop after gross motor skills, a child's muscles generally develop outwards from their trunk and downwards from their shoulders so they develop sitting before standing, reaching before grasping, patting and palmar grip before pincer grip of finger and thumb.

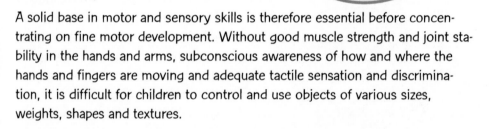

A solid base in motor and sensory skills is therefore essential before concentrating on fine motor development. Without good muscle strength and joint stability in the hands and arms, subconscious awareness of how and where the hands and fingers are moving and adequate tactile sensation and discrimination, it is difficult for children to control and use objects of various sizes, weights, shapes and textures.

The eye muscles also need to work in a co-ordinated way so the child can quickly locate and track objects as well as to guide the hands. It is also essential to be able to motor plan - to organise and carry out a sequence of unfamiliar motor tasks and co-ordinate the two sides of the body.

Water Play: Use different types of sponges to soak and squeeze. There are toys available for water play which require squeezing so the child can shoot at targets. Keep a lookout in the shops. Try water pistols against the wall outside, or thin paint in spray bottles on a cheap shower curtain or wallpaper pinned to the fence.

Peg Games: Different sized clothes pegs are good for developing strength. Think of different ways of opening and closing the clothes pegs - thumb and index, thumb and little finger. Play a game where you hang washing on the line or clip the pegs on to an animal's tail (a piece of string). Place them around the edge of a shoebox or tin and roll a dice. Take off the pegs according to the number of the dice.

Collages: Scrunch up paper to glue on to a bigger picture to develop strength in the hand and fingers. The tearing and ripping of paper is also good for developing a tripod grip, the type that is used to hold a pencil. Practise this in making papier mache or torn paper pictures with tissue paper.

Cotton Reel Printing: If you can find some wooden reels, cut the edges to make patterned printers. Some cotton reels have serrated edges which look attractive when dipped in paint and then rolled or stamped.

Popcorn Shapes: Use a sheet of A4 paper and draw shapes on it. Outline the shape with glue. Place some popcorn or polystyrene 'wiggles' in a tub. The child has to pick up the popcorn and stick it to the shape using a pincer grip. Try letter shapes as well.

String Pictures: Cut some lengths of string and dip them in a mixture of paint and glue. Place these onto card or paper to make patterns and shapes. Or fold a piece of paper over the painty string, press down and pull the string out to make a different pattern. Use different textures of string, wool, threads, nylon, plastic coated.

Pasta Pictures: Cook some spaghetti or pasta shapes (stars are suitably small and fiddly!). Cool and give to children to make pictures and patterns. The pasta will stick to paper with its own starch, so you don't need glue. Adding food colouring to the cooking water makes coloured pasta.

Maracas: Children can make musical maracas by partially filling some plastic bottles with dried peas, lentils or gravel, using a pincer grip or even tweezers! If you offer different fillings and different sizes, types and shapes of containers, you could have a band - playing simple instruments helps fine motor development.

Magic Pictures: Draw a series of shapes, numbers or letters on large pieces of paper with the candle. The image is almost invisible. Using a paintbrush and thin water paint, colour over the wax drawing to reveal a magic picture. Encourage the children to make their own magic images. Also encourage the use of specific strokes when revealing the picture, horizontal, vertical etc, working the strokes to the top/bottom and left and right of the paper.

Frothy Choc: The child measures and pours the milk into a bowl and adds the required milk shake mix. Then, holding the stationary handle of the beater with the non-dominant hand and the rotary handle with the dominant hand, the child rotates the wheel until the milk is frothy (They may need some help to steady the bowl!). Sing 'This is the Way I Make Chocolate Milk' to the tune of 'Here We Go Round the Mulberry Bush' as you whisk.

Dinosaurs: In this activity the child rolls out a length of plasticine starting with a fairly thin sausage. The child then makes dinosaur spikes along the roll by pinching together the plasticine. The thicker the roll the harder it is to pinch. Different textures make the task easier or harder - try playdough, clay, bread dough etc.

Find the Money: Bury small objects to bury such as coins or buttons in a ball of dough. The children 'pluck' at the dough using pincer or tripod grips to find the money. Or bury small objects in sand, jelly, gloop or compost. Try using tweezers or tongs for a change.

Duck Race: You need a water tray, large meat basters, squirters or washing up liquid bottles and a set of plastic ducks. Line up the ducks in the water and squeeze the 'puffer' to send the duck to the finishing post.

Tactile Play

The tactile system is the sense of touch. Through this system we gain information about our world. Tactile discrimination allows us to:

* determine where we are being touched and what is touching us.

It is through tactile exploration (feeling objects with hands mouths and other body parts) that children begin to understand three dimensional objects.

SLIME

What you need:

* soap flakes
* 2 litres warm water
* egg beaters, kitchen gadgets such as a funnel, cup, whisk, soup ladle, scoop, soap drainers, punnets, sponges, jug etc.
* large plastic container
* food colouring (optional)

What you do:

1. The children can help at all stages. Dissolve the soap flakes in warm water in a large plastic container. Add food colouring if desired. Allow mixture to stand until it becomes thick. Add more water if necessary. Beat the mixture with egg beaters.
2. Use kitchen gadgets to pour, measure, scoop, beat and whisk. Children can also use words to describe how the mixture feels and what they are doing.

NOTE: Younger children enjoy slime but need careful supervision and warning to avoid soap getting in their eyes.

MIX AND SORT

What you need:

* large containers of seeds, dried peas, beans, lentils, rice, grains, tea leaves, cereal, pasta shapes etc.
* spoons, scoops, tongs, cup measures and plastic containers for mixing and sorting.

What you do:

1. Arrange containers of seeds in the centre of a table outdoors or in an easy-to-clean area. Give a medium sized container to each child for mixing.
2. Use scoops, spoons, tongs and cups to measure, stir and pour, but don't eat!

FLOATING AND SINKING

What you need:

* Objects which will float or sink - ping pong balls, golf balls, wooden or plastic bricks, kitchen gadgets, sponges, strainers, straws, stones, flowers, corks, confetti, containers of various sizes.
* A large container filled with water
* Food colouring (optional)

What you do:

1. Working outdoors, fill the container with water. Add food colouring to the water if desired.
2. With adult involvement to encourage thinking, watching and discussion, drop the objects into the water and observe floating and sinking. Guess which objects will sink and which will float. Talk about why this happens. Children will also enjoy pouring and squeezing water from sponges and playing with the objects in water.

GOOP

What you need:

* 2 packets of cornflour
* 2 cups of water
* food colouring
* plastic or newspaper covered table, preferably outdoors
* large container
* aprons

What you do:

1. Help the children to mix the water and colouring into the cornflour. The goop should have a thick consistency. Add extra water if necessary.
2. Put on aprons. Plunge hands into the goop and feel the consistency. Use words to describe the feeling: 'sticky, slimy, cool' etc.
3. Enjoy exploring the behaviour of goop; it runs through the fingers, swirls slowly and has a pleasant, heavy feeling. Children can make patterns in the air and on the table.

COLOURED ICE MELTS

What you need:
* food colouring
* water
* plastic containers of various sizes and shapes for freezing
* large plastic containers

What you do:
1. Help the children to add food colouring to water. Freeze the different colours of water in various containers overnight.
2. Look at the patterns formed in the ice by the food colouring. Colour will either freeze evenly or coagulate in patches in the ice.
3. Empty the coloured ice into a large container of water or into an empty container. Watch it melt - colours will mix, swirl and blend together. Dark colours are best added to the bowl last as they will eventually give a murky colour to the water.
4. Feel and watch the shapes of the melting ice and observe the mixing colours. Discuss why it melts. Children also like to touch ice and watch whether it floats or sinks.

COLD SPAGHETTI

What you need:
* Objects which will float or sink - ping pong balls, golf balls, wooden or plastic bricks, kitchen gadgets, sponges, strainers, straws, stones, flowers, corks, confetti, containers of various sizes.
* A large container filled with water
* Food colouring (optional)

What you do:
1. Cook some spaghetti, pasta and rice. Let it go cold. Make collages, bury treasure in it. Or just get the hands in and get mucky!

Self-help Skills

Many children with DCD have difficulty with the sorts of skills which support independence and autonomy. You will probably need to spend more time in planning activities and resources to help individual children to feel confident and competent autonomous learners. Here are some suggestions.

Dressing (General Strategies)

- Knitted fabrics have more elasticity than woven ones and are easier to pull on/take off.
- For some children the experience of having a sweater/polo neck stuck around the forehead can be very frightening, as their vision is obscured. Ensure that non-fastening necklines have sufficient elasticity to allow them to pass easily over their head.
- Raglan, dolman or batwing sleeves allow more room to manoeuvre the arm down the sleeve.
- Any fastening should be at the front of the garment so that it is possible for the child to visually monitor their own hand movements while manipulating the fastenings.
- Some children with DCD are irritated by particular textures and by labels in garments. It may be necessary to cut out labels and consider different types of materials and fabrics.

Dressing (Buttons)

- Some children are only able to do buttons very slowly. It is particularly important that each button is fastened through the correct hole. Help children get into the habit of beginning buttoning at the lower edge of the shirt or blouse so they can see if the corresponding button and button hole have been chosen. This may save the frustration of having to repeat the task because the buttons have been mismatched with their holes!
- Managing buttons begins at around 3-4 years. Children progress from:
    * managing large front buttons to
    * managing small front buttons to
    * cuff and trouser buttons to
    * back buttons.
  Practise with button games before moving on to garments, and remember that some children will need MUCH more practice than others.

Using the toilet

Many children find bottom-wiping difficult at this age, and some children with DCD have additional problems due to their poor balance The problem with loos is that:

Toilets are often adult size (except in Nursery/Infant Schools) and the child can't get their feet to the floor, which is necessary for balance. Also in order to wipe their bottom the child needs to lean over their sitting base and transfer their weight forward in order to leave a space behind to use the toilet paper. If their feet do not reach the floor they will find this hard to do.

Try the following:

a) Use a toilet inset

b) Use a small step or block so that the child's feet are on a firm surface.

When wiping their bottoms children need to know where their hands are when they go behind their backs. Children with motor difficulties or learning difficulties often need to monitor what they are doing with their eyes, and the task of wiping their bottoms is hard for them. They either avoid the task or try and then get into a mess. To help them understand and feel where their hands are, play games where they have to pass a ball or bean bag around their middle and through their legs, forwards and backwards.

Eating and Drinking

When we think of co-ordination skills we tend to think of the big skills like running, jumping and balancing, as well as fine motor skills for holding objects and manipulating toys. Co-ordination also affects other muscles, for example those in the tongue and the lips, which can affect feeding and drinking skills.

A child with DCD may have problems managing different textures in their mouth. The may appear fussy with their food, preferring to eat foods that require little or no chewing, preferring melt in the mouth food such as yogurt, crisps or chocolate. They may have difficulty co-ordinating the action for swallowing and may appear to cough or choke a lot at snack and drinks time.

At mealtimes they have to control the spoon when lifting the food off the plate and accurately getting it to their mouth with the minimum spillage. While many young children may still find this a little hard, the DCD child finds it harder, often resorting to using their fingers. They may also have poor awareness of how much food is in their mouth and around their lips. Again, whilst this still can be common for children of this age, these things do remain an issue for these children as they grow up and if not addressed early on can have a huge social impact as they develop.

In order to overcome some of these difficulties:

- 🖐 to maximise control of their arms, children need to be able to maintain a stable posture. With the exception of specific nursery or infant schools, most dining room chairs are too far off the ground for a child to put their feet on the floor. Children will be seen either:
  - * slouching back in the chair, making it harder to use their hands because they are so far away, or
  - * leaning heavily with their tummy or forearms into the table top to support themselves, or
  - * anchoring their elbows in order to try to control their hands because they find it too difficult to use their arms freely away from their body. Anchoring makes it very difficult to move fluently and often means items are spilt or cutlery is not used or improperly managed.
- 🖐 Try raising their feet on an upturned firm box and pushing their bottom nearer the front of the seat by placing a firm cushion(s) behind their back.
- 🖐 Check that the child can reach the table and does not have to reach up as this will make them tired very quickly.
- 🖐 A firm block of foam is better to sit on than a cushion.
- 🖐 Use chairs with arms on the sides or use a child's table and chair set. An adjustable chair may need to be considered, see resources for such as a 'Trip Trap' chair.
- 🖐 Once the child is sitting in a stable position, encourage them to try to use both hands, e.g. one hand holding cutlery and one hand holding the plate or holding a spoon in one hand and fork in the other hand.

- be aware of the texture, mix and temperature of food, and check for individual preferences with the child's family;
- look at the type of cutlery available - short chunky handles may be better. Alternatively, modify spoons and forks by bending the neck of the fork or spoon slightly inwards. A moulded set of cutlery such as 'Caring Cutlery' is useful for children who find it hard to hold and manipulate knifes, forks and spoons (see resources);
- use deeper dishes so the child can use the sides to help push the food onto the spoon/fork;
- put non-slip matting under dishes and plates to stop them slipping about on the table - a piece of damp cloth under the item will also work;
- don't put too much liquid in cups;
- offer straws for drinks - the sucking action is good exercise for their mouth muscles.

Early Organisation Skills

The ability to sequence and organise enables us to orientate ourselves in time and space, and is a key problem for children with DCD as they grow up. The Foundation Stage offers a prime opportunity to begin to develop these skills.

The development of sequencing ability follows a general progression in the following order:
- sequencing of movement;
- sequencing of events throughout the day;
- sequencing of symbols in numbers and letters;
- sequencing of time.

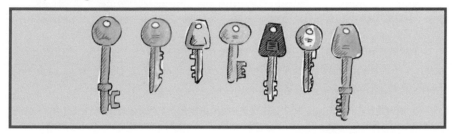

Some general ideas to help develop organisational skills:

- help the child to identify the steps needed to begin and accomplish the task;
- ask the child questions about what they are going to do and how, where and who they are going to do it with;
- encourage the child to verbalise what they are doing while carrying out the activity;
- designate a place or container for each belonging;
- practise gross motor activities that require sequences of movement. Dance, rhythm and music are all excellent for this;
- link sequencing activities to language and maths aspects of the foundation phase e.g. patterns;
- use timers to alert the child to the beginning and end of an activity;
- establish routines and be consistent.

Visual Time Tables

A daily schedule is a timetable, and a point of reference, to let children know what activities will occur and in what sequence.

These timetables can be used for different ability levels using a variety of media:

1. Objects to represent activities (a swimming costume, a football)
2. Photos of activities and people (assembly, story time, a parent helper)
3. Pictures drawn by the child or an adult (people. places, things)
4. Symbols (either from a formal system such as Makaton or invented ones)
5. Written, sometimes in a timetable form (with words, signs, numbers, times etc)

Use them at the start of the week and each day to reinforce what is going to happen. These timetables can be broken down further to be used as task components if teaching a new skill, for example, dressing. These can be produced on small cards which the child can be encouraged to sequence, then action.

Coping with Overload

Children with DCD can often become overloaded and over-stimulated in your environment. In the early years setting the environment is bright and stacked with visual stimuli, the day is very full and this can become just too much for them.

Overload may manifest itself in tantrums, labile moods (swinging from laughing to crying) or stubbornness. Our temptation may be to console the child, or to try and get them to continue to engage in what is going on.

At this point the children are stressed and unable to benefit from the help you are offering. They need some time out - just like us when we have had a bad day at work and need 'Just five minutes peace and quiet'.

> Some children with DCD can become stressed and may need time out.

Here are some strategies to add to your tool box!

- Provide a quiet space - this could be the Home Corner with lots of pillows and a blanket, or the book corner. Make sure the child knows that they can retreat to this place at any time.
- Create a sensory room with a soothing and calming atmosphere. Use soft lights, block out distractions, have big bean bags and soft fabrics the child can snuggle into. Add some soft toys and coloured lights.
- Play some calming music.
- Play some 'cool down games' such as Sleeping lions, or teach simple relaxation techniques to the whole group.
- Have a story - you could let the child sit by themselves at the back, perhaps sitting in a bean bag or on their own special chair.

Where to go for Further Advice

At this age, children will have access to a number of professionals concerned with their developmental progress, and any concerns can be discussed with them. Parents and practitioners can also access the Local Authority advisory services or psychology services. Many of the staff here are specially trained in the area of DCD. You could also encourage the parents to approach their GP for a referral to the local Child Development Centre.

There are a number of local support groups, but the following contacts are particularly useful:

A charitable organisation set up to provide information and advice.

> Dyspraxia Foundation
> 8 West Alley, Hitchin, Herts SG5 1EG
> Tel; 01462 454986
> Fax: 01462 455052
> www.embrook.demon.co.uk/dyspraxia/

An independent service consisting of a multi-agency team of health and education professionals who can offer assessment and information on Specific Learning Difficulties, training and products.

> Dyscovery Centre
> Tel:02920 628222
> Fax: 029 20628333
> E-mail: dyscoverycentre@btclick.com
> www.dyscovery.co.uk

Books

There are a number of books available on the subject of DCD, but there is relatively little for children in the early years setting, mainly due to the nature of the developing child. Some references are given below:

Dyspraxia - The Hidden Handicap; Dr. Amanda Kirby; ISBN 0-28563512-3

Guide to Dyspraxia and Developmental Co-ordination Disorders; Amanda Kirby & Sharon Drew; ISBN 1-85346-913-0

Dyspraxia in the Early Years; Christine Macintyre; ISBN 1-85346-677-8

Enhancing Learning Through Play; Christine McIntyre; ISBN 1-85346-761-8

Movement and Learning in the Early Years; Christine McIntyre & Kim McVitty;
ISBN 1-4129-0237-1

Making Inclusion Work for Children with Dyspraxia; Gill Dixon & Lois M Addy;
ISBN 0-415-31489-5

Who's who in multi-agency working?

The following professionals are likely to be involved with the assessment, treatment and remediation of children with motor co-ordination difficulties:

Pediatrician/school doctor

A hospital or community-based children's doctor, often specialising in children with special needs.

Physiotherapist (PTs)

PTs are concerned with the child's gross motor development, especially in relation to PE and physical play. They too can advise on games and activities to develop movement skills.

Educational Psychologist (EPs)

are concerned with the child's educational/cognitive development.

Advisory Teachers

ATs are usually based within the Local Authority. They have special expertise in a variety of special needs. They support the staff in settings in meeting the needs of children who may have difficulty in accessing learning activities.

Occupational Therapist (OTs)

OTs are concerned with developing practical every day living strategies for children, such as self-help skills of dressing, social skills, play skills. They can offer ideas and activities to develop these skills as well as advising on adaptation of equipment, toys or games that might be required.

Speech & Language Therapists (SALTs)

SALTs are concerned with different aspects of language and communication, including expressive and receptive language, non-verbal language and social skills.

Special Educational Needs Co-ordinators (SENCOs)

A SENCO is usually a member of the staff who has a special interest in children with special needs. They can assist practitioners and teachers in developing strategies to support children in the educational settings.

Professionals from Social services and Sure Start may also be involved.

Working together

Collaborative working is vital for children who may be identified as having special educational or additional needs.

Characteristics of effective partnerships

- Early referral from health to education and vice versa.
- Open door access to both school and health facilities.
- Multi professional/parent observation at assessment.
- Multi professional/parent discussions about services.
- Mutual acceptance of changes in professional 'power' in varying settings.
- Attendance at both formal and informal reviews.
- Written confirmation of advice and agreed action.
- Regular and reliable contact between parents and professionals.
- Opportunities for training and information sharing.

Key Points to Remember:

- ☺ DCD presents with a variety of features - only rarely will two children present the same.
- ☺ DCD is a specific learning difficulty and often overlaps with other conditions such as dyslexia and ADHD.
- ☺ Children with DCD are generally average or above average intelligence.
- ☺ Children with DCD do not grow out of it. Self-esteem and confidence are major problems for them as they grow up. Academic performance is usually affected by the condition.
- ☺ There is no magic cure for DCD. However, children can be helped through understanding and practical support to meet their needs.
- ☺ Observe the child over a variety of activities and across a period of time. Keep records - not only about what they appear to find hard to do but also how they are doing it.
- ☺ Parents, teachers and health professionals should work together in partnership to provide a consistent approach and make best use of available resources.

Useful Resources

Apparatus
Direction Hands and Feet
Motor Skills Universal Set
Primary Games Kit
Mega Scoots or Roll Around
Tail balls
Bean bag scarves
Frog/dog bean bags
Kick-a-Flick
Space Hoppers
Ribbons on Sticks
Tactile Stepping Stones

Davies Sports
Findel House
Excelsior Road
Ashby-de-la-Zouch
Leicestershire
Tel: 0845 120 4515
www.daviessport.co.uk

Movement Programmes for the Foundation Stage:

Smart Moves by Sharon Drew

Smart Coaching & Consultancy
37 Mill Street
Usk; Monmouthshire
NP15 1AP
Tel: 01291 673926
email: enquiries@smartc.c.co.uk

Fundamentals - Movement Ideas for the Early Years

Gymnastic Enterprises Ltd
Unit 1
Lilleshall hall Farm Road
Newport, Shropshire
TF10 9AS
www.earlyyearsfundamentals.co.uk

Non Slip Matting - Dycem

Nottingham Rehab Supplies (NRS)
Novara House
Excelsior Road
Ashby-de-la-Zouch, Leicestershire
LE65 1NG
Tel: 0845 120 4522
www.nrs-uk.co.uk

OR
Homecraft Ability One
PO Box 5665
Kirkby in Ashfield
Nottinghamshire
NG17 7QX
Tel: 08702 423305
www.homecraftabilityone.com

More Useful Resources

Developing Scissors Skills

Books:
Cutting Skills by Mark & Katy Hill

Developing Basic Scissor Skills by Sue Mahoney & Alison Markwell

Specialist scissors from

Writing
Write from the Start **by Lois Addy**

Write Dance - **a music and movement approach to developing writing**

Adjustable Seating
Trip Trap Chair

Books of Ideas and Activities
The Little Book of Dough
The Little Book of Nursery Rhymes
The Little Book of Playground Games
We Can Do It - Independent Learning in the Foundation Stage

LDA
Abbeygate House
East Road
Cambridge
CB1 1DB
Tel: 0845 120 4776
www.ldalearning.com

PETA (UK) LTD
Mark's Hall
Mark's Hall Lane
Margaret Roding
Dunmow
CM6 1QT
Tel: 01245 231118
www.peta-uk.com

LDA as above

LUCKY DUCK PUBLISHING
3 Thorndale mews
Clifton, Bristol
Tel: 0117 9732881
www.luckyduck.co.uk

Back in Action
43 Woodside Road
Amersham-on-the-Hill
Buckingham
HP6 6AA
Tel: 01494 434343
www.backinaction.co.uk

Featherstone Education
44 High Street
Husbands Bosworth
Leicestershire
LE17 6LP
Tel: 01858 881213
www.featherstone.uk.com

Other titles in this series

Including Children with:

Attention and Behaviour Difficulties (ABD)
by Maureen Garner

Autistic Spectrum Disorders (ASD)
by Clare Beswick

Down's Syndrome
by Clare Beswick

Asperger's Syndrome
By Clare Beswick

Coming soon

Working within the P Levels
by Kay Holman and Janet Beckett

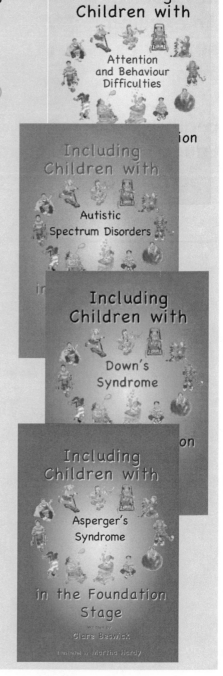

Including
Children with

Attention
and Behaviour
Difficulties

Including
Children with

Autistic
Spectrum Disorders

Including
Children with

Down's
Syndrome

Including
Children with

Asperger's
Syndrome

in the Foundation
Stage

Written by
Clare Beswick

Illustrated by Martha Hardy